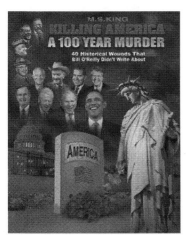

© 2015   M S KING

*"History is indeed little more than the register of the crimes, follies and misfortunes of mankind."*

**Edward Gibbon, English historian (1737-1794)**

**From:** *"The Decline and Fall of the Roman Empire"*

# About the Author

Based in the New York City area, M. S. King is a private investigative journalist and researcher. A 1987 graduate of Rutgers University, King's subsequent career in Marketing & Advertising has equipped him with a unique perspective when it comes to understanding how "public opinion" is indeed scientifically manufactured.

Madison Ave marketing acumen combines with 'City Boy' instincts to make M.S. King one of the most tenacious detectors of "things that don't add up" in the world today. Says King of his admitted quirks, irreverent disdain for "conventional wisdom", and uncanny ability to ferret out and weave together important data points that others miss: *"Had Sherlock Holmes been an actual historical personage, I would have been his reincarnation."*

King is also the author of:

- *The War Against Putin: What the Government-Media Complex Isn't Telling You About Russia.*
- *The Bad War: The Story Never Taught About World War 2*
- *The Real Roosevelts: What Ken Burns & PBS Didn't Tell You*

King's other interests include: the animal kingdom, philosophy, chess, cooking, literature and history *(with emphasis on events of the late 19th through the 20th centuries).*

# INTRODUCTION

FOX Host Bill O'Reilly is known for his "Killing" books in which he writes about historical figures who have died under controversial circumstances. There is 'Killing Lincoln", "Killing Kennedy", "Killing Patton", and "Killing Jesus". But the one killing that O'Reilly has yet to write about - or perhaps we should say, *is not allowed to* write about - is the killing of America. Make no mistake; the America we once knew has indeed been murdered.

By now, most Americans, regardless of their political persuasion, have come to realize that something is not quite right in America. You may not be able to put your finger on it, but you sense it instinctively.

How can you *not* sense it? For the first time ever, both the majority of the younger and the older generations of America now believe that future generations will not be as prosperous as their parents' generation was. And that's only the economic pessimism. On the social and cultural fronts, how many of us can truly say that we are proud are what our society has degenerated to?

How did we arrive at this point of perpetual debt, perpetual inflation, massive taxation, chronically high unemployment, disintegrating families, massive dependency on the state, perpetual war, and ever-worsening moral degeneracy, mass psychological depression, and cultural degradation?

Who did it? Why did they do it? How did they do it? How was the 'murder' concealed from the American people?

Through the use of 40 clear, concise and very easy to digest illustrated 'blurbs' *(The 40 Wounds),* **Killing America**: **The 100 Year Murder** will answer those questions for you. This is a mass-distribution booklet designed for 'crash-course' simplicity. Please share it with others.

# AMERICA: 1900

**McKinley Election Poster (1900)**

It is the dawn of the 20th Century. In just over a century's time, the United States of America has grown from a sparsely populated group of post-colonial States into the richest, strongest, most virtuous and happiest nation on earth. During this time, America has overcome a devastating Civil War and the painful post-war Southern Reconstruction.

From "sea to shining sea", America's industrial cities, bustling ports, rich farms, and world class Universities are the envy of the modern world. America's population *(now about 80 million)* is upwardly mobile and highly literate. The Middle Class is booming as opportunity-seeking European immigrants clamor to get in. America's Black population, though only a generation removed from slavery and still segregated, is also making undeniable material and cultural progress.

In this rapidly developing "land of opportunity" there are no Federal Income Taxes, no State Income Taxes, no Sales Taxes, no Social Security Taxes, no Capital Gains Taxes, no IRS, no Department of Homeland Security, no Department of Education, no welfare schemes, no Central Bank, very little debt, and a sound currency backed by Gold.

There are no limits for a free people enjoying the fruits of a free market, an honest currency, and a government strictly limited in its size and power. In the fresh air of liberty, invention and innovation thrive. The list of history changing American inventors produced in this environment is indeed astonishing: Robert Fulton *(Steam Boat)*, Eli Whitney *(Cotton Gin)*, Thomas Edison *(Modern Light Bulb & Phonograph to name a few)*, Serbian-American Nicola Tesla *(Commercial Electricity)*, Cyrus McCormick *(Mechanical Reaper)*, Alexander Graham Bell *(Telephone)*, The Wright Brothers *(Airplane)*, and many more.

On the cultural front, American artists and literary figures are gaining wide renown, impressing even the more culturally advanced Europeans. Names like Mark Twain, Herman Melville, and Edgar Allen Poe rank with Europe's finest writers.

*Edison – Tesla – Twain*

In foreign commerce and relations, Americans are a peace-loving people who have no interest in embroiling their young country in Europe's intrigues and squabbles. The idea of going overseas to fight foreign 'bogeymen' is unthinkable.

America's prosperity affords many of its people the luxury of increasing leisure time. From this free time grow Sports Leagues such as Baseball's National League (1876), to be followed by the American League (1901). College Football has exploded in popularity, with the first professional teams to form in the early years of the new century. Millions of young men sharpen their bodies and mental toughness by competing in all varieties of Sports.

As for the women folk, the ladies of America are exactly that, ladies. Women are family oriented, valued for their sweet demeanor, and respected for their virtue. If a young American buck expects to get intimate with a young lady, he had better grow up, get a job and marry the lass, lest her daddy chase him off with a shotgun!

America's children are raised to respect their God, their parents, their elders, and their teachers. Mouthing off to the teacher would get you smacked upside the head, and then again when your parents found out.

Underpinning America's foundation of tiny government, free enterprise, and peaceful commerce, is the commonly practiced Christian morality, self-control, industriousness, and true goodness of the American people. Grown children take care of their elderly parents and other relatives. Strong families, active churches, and community groups take care of the unfortunate. Government welfare is neither needed, nor desired.

*1: 1900 Poster extols the popular President McKinley, the Gold Currency Standard, and the American prosperity of "The Gilded Age"*

*2: America's economy attracts many fine European immigrants. Unfortunately, some Reds and gangsters also arrive.*

*3: Manufacturing jobs are available for anyone who wants to work.*

As "The Gay Nineties" *('gay' as in happy!)* draw to a close, America the Beautiful seems poised to prosper for centuries to come. With the new technologies and industrial advances to come *(automobiles, electricity etc.)*, there is no telling what new heights of universal happiness and prosperity await the lucky inhabitants of the young and confident Republic.

But way beneath the surface, invisible to most, a well-funded and well-organized "Advance Guard" of termites has been arriving in America since the 1880's. These "Reds", aka "Marxists", aka "The Left", aka "Progressives", bring with them the disease of "liberalism" that has already been plaguing Europe since the days of the French Revolution. Their long-range plan is to sow discord, undermine the American way of life and system of limited government, and to erect a highly centralized system of 'Global Governance" in its place.

In order to grow their ranks, Red leaders cleverly and skillfully exploit some of the legitimate imperfections of America, particularly in regard to industrial labor conditions and banking practices. About the turn of the century, Jewish Money Kings such as Jacob Schiff and Bernard Baruch are already joining forces with power hungry, Anglo-American Money Kings like JP Morgan and John D Rockefeller. The Globalist Money Kings "in the suites" will use the Red agitators "in the streets" to slowly change a free, virtuous, prosperous, and peaceful Republic, into the centrally controlled, degenerate, bankrupt, and warmongering cesspool that is modern-day America under Barack Obama.

*Early architects of 'The New World Order': Schiff, Rockefeller, Morgan, Baruch*

### So, America, what the heck happened?!

It's all very simple! Step into our fast-moving time machine and let us briefly review "the Forty Wounds that Killed America."

## WOUND # 1: 1896
## Adolph Ochs Buys 'The New York Times'

### What Happened?

The most influential newspaper in America is purchased by a wealthy Zionist-Leftist.

### Consequence

Ochs' descendants (*the Ochs-Sulzberger Family*) control The Times to this day, Worshipped by many as "the paper of record", The immensely powerful Times has been manipulating public opinion in favor of big-spending liberalism, aggressive Globalism and Zionism *(pro-Israel)* for 120 year now, and counting.

Once dubbed by the writer Gore Vidal as "the Typhoid Mary of American journalism", the misinformed public opinion manufactured by the Sulzberger-Ochs gang influences all other media in America.

*Lefty Adolph Ochs (left) and his Great Grandson Arthur Sulzberger (who controls The Times today).*

## What Happened?

On September 6, 1901, President McKinley is shot at close range by a Red *(Communist/Anarchist)* named Leon Czolgosz. McKinley dies one week later.

## Consequence:

The assassination makes Vice President Teddy Roosevelt (TR) the new President. Unlike the conservative McKinley *(who had TR forced upon him after his 1st VP died)*, the left-leaning TR was an advocate of big, centralized government and aggressive foreign policy. **TR ushers in the "Progressive Era".** This moment in history marks the acceleration of America's transition from a peaceful limited Republic into a socialistic globe-trotting foreign menace.

In 1908, TR's "National Monetary Commission" sets the stage for the eventual 1913 founding of a U.S. Central Bank under fellow progressive Woodrow Wilson, a scoundrel whose destructive Presidency will have been made possible by TR's deliberate interference in the 1912 Presidential election.

*1: Red Czolgosz shoots McKinley at close range.*

*2: Czolgosz is a devotee of "Red Emma" Goldman, who praises the killing!*

*3: The murder of McKinley catapults the warmongering Left Progressive TR into power.*

## WOUND # 3: 1909
## The N.A.A.C.P. Is Established

### What Happened?

Ostensibly set up to help Blacks, the National Association for the Advancement of Colored People *(N.A.A.C.P.)* is founded by a group of wealthy Jewish Marxists. They select a Black Communist front-man named W.E. DuBois.

### Consequence

Slowly but surely, the N.A.A.C.P. steers millions of Blacks away from the conservative, inspirational influence of Booker T. Washington and herds them into the Marxist-Democrat political camp instead. A 100 year diet of anti-White victimization propaganda creates a blind voting bloc that is now 95% Democrat. **The leverage of the organized, controlled Black vote is a key element of Big Government Marxism in America.** Ironically, as we shall explore later on, Democrat liberal policies will inflict enormous harm upon American Black families.

*The philosophy of conservative Black leader Booker T Washington (left), was undermined by Jewish Marxist N.A.A.C.P. Board members such as Red international banker Jacob Schiff (center) and the Communist puppet front man, W.E. DuBois (right).*

# WOUND # 4: 1913
## The 17th Amendment *(Direct Election of U.S. Senators)*

## What Happened?

U.S. Senators will no longer be appointed by State legislatures *(as the Constitution stipulates)*. All Senators must now run for election and re-election every 6 years.

## Consequence

Senators soon become controllable creatures of Washington DC-based national politics. To win elections, future Senators will have to answer to national political bosses and media created "public opinion", not to their individual States. **This is a major step towards the consolidation of power away from the States, and into the hands of a super-centralized Federal government in Washington DC.**

*The direct election of Senators means that many respected and duly appointed Statesmen will eventually be replaced by attention-seeking political whores.*

# WOUND # 5: 1913
## The Income Tax *(The Revenue Act)*

### What Happened?

Less than one year into the Presidency of Woodrow Wilson, low income tax rates of 1 - 6% are imposed only upon the wealthy. Assurances are given that the rates will never increase and that only the wealthy will have to pay this new tax.

### Consequence

Contrary to the original promises, Income Tax rates not only skyrocket as the years pass, but the brackets expand downward to entrap middle and lower income workers as well. Unlimited access to the paychecks of millions of American workers fuels the growth of liberty-destroying Big Government at home and never-ending foreign wars abroad.

*The headache and wealth loss of the annual I.R.S. shake-down serves only to fund America's war machine and the parasitic permanent welfare underclass.*

# WOUND # 6: 1913
## The Federal Reserve Act

## What Happened?

Two months after the Income Tax is passed, a privately owned, New York based Banking Mafia *(The Fed)* is given the privilege of controlling the issuance of America's currency, ***at interest.***

## Consequence

Under the unseen leadership of German-Jewish banker Paul Warburg, the Federal Reserve System soon exceeds its original mandate to act as "lender of last resort" for undercapitalized banks. The Central Bank initiates a 100 year period of constant inflation, massive deficits *(financed in part by the Fed's printed money)*, recessions, depressions, stock market manipulations, secret bailouts, destructive asset bubbles, and un-payable mountains of consumer debt.

The private Fed Mafia, and its political, academic, and media allies, will thwart all future attempts to either reign in its power, or to simply audit its books.

*1: Paul Warburg (Left) and 2: JP Morgan (Right) are two of the powerful men behind the Fed.*

*3: Period cartoon warns of the dangers of "The Coming Money Trust"*

*4: Modern day cartoon depicts recent Fed Chairman Bernanke throwing debt-based paper money out of a helicopter.*

# WOUND # 7: 1917 - 1919
## World War I

## What Happened?

As Germany pleads with Britain & France to make peace, President Wilson tricks America into a senseless war that will alter the course of history, for the worse. More than 100,000 Americans are killed in 1918 alone.

## Consequence

The dangerous precedent of involving America in major overseas wars is firmly established as American entry turns the tide of war against Germany, Austria-Hungary, and the Ottoman Empire *(Turkey)*.

The inhumane terms of the infamous Treaty of Versailles which follows set the stage for a future, even bloodier World War 20 years later. World War I also leads to the British takeover of Palestine and massive Jewish immigration to that land. In decades to come, the resulting Arab-Israeli conflict will create many problems for America.

*1: Progressive / Zionist Puppet Woodrow Wilson drags the U.S. into war.*

*2: Zionist Fred Strothman's iconic anti-German propaganda poster*

*3: American boys are played for fools and shipped off to die.*

## What Happened?

The U.S. Constitution is amended to guarantee voting privileges to women in every State of America.

## Consequence

Exactly as the cunning proponents of Big Government had anticipated, a "feminized" American electorate becomes easier to manipulate with emotion-based appeals to security, fear, and sympathy. The liberty-killing growth of "the nanny state" is largely fueled by soft-hearted, but misguided female voters and their delicate "feelings" towards "the poor", "the elderly", "the children", "the minorities", "the illegal immigrants" etc.

*1: Suffragettes march for their 'voting rights'*

*2:  Not every man is in favor of the idea.*

## WOUND # 9: 1926
## David Sarnoff Establishes NBC

### What Happened?

RCA Radio General Manager David Sarnoff, the son of Russian-Jewish immigrants, forms NBC Radio.

### Consequence

Sarnoff and his children will reign over the NBC radio *(and later TV)* Empire for more than 50 years. NBC News and NBC TV Shows will promote the Globalist Left's agenda, making Sarnoff one of the most influential opinion molders of the 20th century.

*The David Sarnoff Family and their million dollar radio & TV mouthpieces will pump out disinformation for many decades to come.*

## What Happened?

Young William Paley Meyer, the son of Jewish immigrants, gains majority ownership of CBS Radio.

## Consequence

Paley will reign over the CBS radio *(and later TV)* Empire for more than 60 years. Like Sarnoff's NBC, CBS News and CBS TV Shows will promote the Globalist Left's agenda, making Paley one of the most influential opinion molders of the 20th century.

*William Paley's agent, CBS Anchor Walter Cronkite, once openly stated that he had always supported World Government.*

*During the 1970's, Paley's 'All in the Family" made a deliberate mockery of the American conservatism of "Archie Bunker". His "60 Minutes" was, and still is, liberal propaganda masquerading as "news".*

## WOUND # 11: 1933
## Eugene Meyer Buys The Washington Post

### What Happened?

Liberal-Zionist Eugene Meyer steps down as Chairman of the Federal Reserve so that he can buy The Washington Post.

### Consequence

Meyer and his descendants *(the Meyer-Graham Family)* will control The Post for the next 80 years. Second only to The New York Times in press power and influence, The Post has been misdirecting public opinion, and directly influencing DC politicians, for 80 years.

*Eugene Meyer (left) and his daughter Katherine (Graham) helped to bend the political thinking of the 20th Century towards the Globalist Left.*

*"Nothing can be believed which is seen in a newspaper. Truth itself becomes suspicious by being put into that polluted vehicle."*

*-Thomas Jefferson, 1807*

# WOUND # 12: 1929-1936
## Great Depression & The New Deal

## What Happened?

Upon replacing the scapegoat Herbert Hoover as President, Franklin Delano Roosevelt (FDR) wastes billions of dollars on welfare and 'make work' schemes. Contrary to current popular belief, these programs neither end, nor even mitigate the Great Depression, which itself was induced by the Fed's deliberate crashing of the Stock Market in 1929.

## Consequence

A dangerous legal and psychological precedent is established. It is during this difficult period in America's history that many people came to view the role of government as a material provider, instead of as the defender of liberty and property. Though economic recovery finally came after World War II; the 'Nanny State' mentality remains to this day.

*The grinning con man's schemes are exposed in "New Deal Or Raw Deal?"*
*By Burton Folsom Jr.*

# WOUND # 13: 1933
## The Social Security Pyramid Scheme

## What Happened?

FDR promises the people that a forced savings plan with dollar for dollar employer matching *("a shoebox")* will be there for them in old age.

## Consequence

Social Security taxes are used to pay current recipients. **There is no "shoebox"!** Every American senior citizen has therefore been cheated out of what would have been a small fortune. **Just imagine what nearly 50 years of employee-employer forced savings, at a reasonable rate of compound growth, would have accumulated to in our "shoeboxes".**

Instead, the monstrous program itself is now busting America's budget, and can only be kept afloat by high SS taxes and currency debasement caused by the Fed's printed money loans to the "SS Trust Fund".

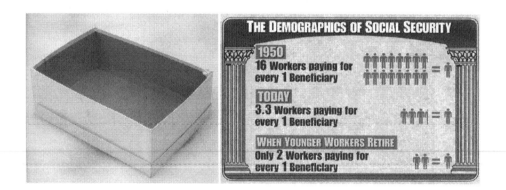

*The 'shoebox' is empty! It was a Pyramid Scheme all along.*

# WOUND # 14: 1941-1945
## World War II

## What Happened?

As Germany continues to plead for peace *(it's true!)*, FDR tricks America into a senseless war that will alter the course of history, for the worse. More than 400,000 Americans are killed.

## Consequence

The aftermath of U.S. involvement in World War II spawns the multi-trillion dollar Cold War *(against a Soviet Union that the U.S. had just saved from extinction.)*, the multi-trillion dollar Military-Industrial complex, multi-billion dollar foreign aid schemes, the war making U.N., the Korean War *(50,000 dead Americans)*, the Vietnam War *(50,000 more dead Americans)*, the nation wrecking IMF and World Bank, NATO, **perpetual Global Policing** and the Israel-Middle East problem.

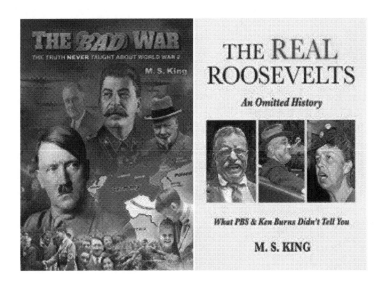

*MUST READING!*

*'The Bad War', and 'The REAL Roosevelts', both by M S King, tell the real story of the Roosevelts and World War II.*

## WOUND # 15: 1945
## The Atomic Bombings of Japan

### What Happened?

As Japan tries desperately to negotiate a surrender *(true story!)*, President Harry Truman orders the atomic bombing of Hiroshima, Japan. A few days later, a 2nd atomic bomb was dropped over Nagasaki.

### Consequence

Though not as deadly as the fire-bombings of Tokyo and Dresden, **the dropping of two atomic bombs on the women, elderly and children of Hiroshima and Nagasaki marks the point in history in which America lost its soul.** Whereas the many other World War II bombings of civilians were downplayed by the Press and never fully realized by the public, the A-Bomb attacks were *known* for what they were, and universally accepted and even *celebrated*.

From that time forward, the regard for innocent human life was never the same in America. From LBJ's saturation bombing of Vietnam, to Bill Clinton's massacre at Waco, TX, to the Bushes' brutal bombings of Iraq, to Obama's Predator Drone murders in places like Yemen or Pakistan, all that is needed to justify genocide is for the U.S. government-media complex to claim that it was necessary to "defend freedom". This moral sickness and callous disregard for human life traces directly back to Truman's holocaust of Hiroshima and Nagasaki.

*Dirty Harry Truman threatens more Atomic genocide with a "Rain of Ruin". Americans knew what happened and still celebrated the "Victory".*

## WOUND # 16: 1940-1960
## Marxists Consolidate Control over Hollywood

### What Happened?

By 1947, concern over the Red infiltration of Hollywood is such that the House Un-American Activities Committee *(HUAC)* holds hearings into the matter. A handful of mainly Jewish writers, producers, and actors are exposed as Communists and then "blacklisted" by the studios. But the 'Big Boys' remain untouched.

### Consequence

Working hand in hand with their News Media brethren, the Marxist Moguls of Hollywood have skillfully manipulated the attitudes, opinions, and behavior of the American masses. A steady diet of subtle, embedded Left propaganda, pornography, homosexuality, and idiocy has inflicted enormous damage upon the American mind and soul.

*The Communist "Hollywood 10" catch some flak, but Hollywood's Red Moguls survive and grow stronger. Their films will corrupt and propagandize three generations of unsuspecting Americans.*

## WOUND # 17: 1943
## IRS Offers Incentives for Employer-Provided Health Insurance

### What Happened?

As a "temporary" wartime measure, employers are given tax incentives for providing a portion of employee compensation in the form of health insurance. Years later, in 1954, these tax advantages are made even sweeter. The government "hook" is set, and the unsuspecting fish, (preoccupied with the war) takes the bait.

### Consequence

The critical market connection between the direct buyer *(patients)* and direct sellers *(hospitals, doctors, insurance companies etc)* is severed. Patients no longer care about the cost of health care because "someone else" is paying.

**This IRS scheme, combined with the explosion of frivolous lawsuits 40 years later, will become the main factors driving up health care costs in America.**

The cunning Left will skillfully use the "crisis" of expensive health care costs as the excuse needed to take over the entire Health Care industry.

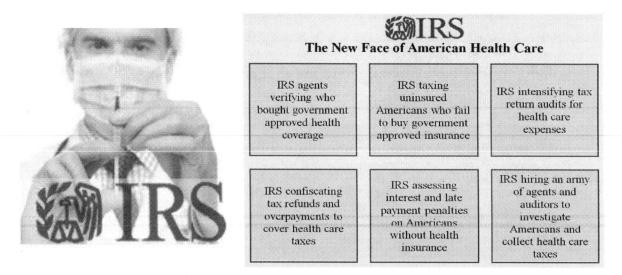

*The long process leading up to ObamaCare's IRS-enforced power-grab began with harmless sounding IRS regulations in 1943.*

### What Happened?

Under the phony pretext of "keeping America safe", the Central Intelligence Agency is established. Americans are told that this spy agency will only operate on foreign soil.

### Consequence

In service to the World Government movement, the CIA operates in many foreign nations as well as domestically. The Agency's main functions include assassinations, false flag terror attacks, and the spreading of strategic disinformation. **The CIA works very closely with media moguls to distort the news and manipulate public opinion.** Its deceptive tentacles reach deep into American academic, financial, and cultural life as well.

*1: In spite of some good agents, the CIA is not your friend! Dark elements within the Agency subvert governments, influence U.S. elections, and works with the mass media to manipulate public opinion.*

*2: CNN anchor and admitted homosexual Anderson Cooper interned at the CIA while in college. He is just one of the many prominent journalists who peddle CIA fairy tales to gullible TV viewers.*

*3: Famous Washington Post journalist Carl Bernstein actually wrote about the CIA's cooperation with and influence over the news media.*

# WOUND # 19: 1953 – 1960
## The 'Progressive' Republican President Eisenhower Castrates the G.O.P. From Within

### What Happened?

Under the 8-year Presidency of Dwight D Eisenhower *(a former Democrat, FDR lover, and Stalin admirer)* the Republican Party makes a sharp leftward Globalist turn. Conservative Republicans are deliberately undermined by 'Ike', whose indifference towards them helps the Democrats to win many seats in the House and Senate.

### Consequence

Apart from the 1964 Barry Goldwater uprising, the once conservative, constitutionalist G.O.P. has been a pro-big government, Globalist-controlled entity ever since. The few exceptions are marginalized by the Party's "moderate" leaders and condemned by the Left media as "extremists". In essence, Ike's killing of the true Republican Party made America a One-Party state.

*As FDR's commanding General during World War II, Democrat Eisenhower engineered the deliberate starvation and disease deaths of 1.5 million German prisoners, and eagerly delivered Eastern Europe into Joe Stalin. Image 2 shows 'Ike' celebrating atop Lenin's tomb with Stalin.*

*As President, the "ex-Democrat" again serves the Globalist Left by greatly weakening the traditional conservative faction of the Republican Party.*

# WOUND # 20: 1953
## Leonard Goldenson Takes Over ABC

### What Happened?

ABC is on the brink of bankruptcy when Liberal-Zionist Leonard Goldenson steps in with a $25 million dollar cash infusion.

### Consequence

Goldenson will reign over the ABC Empire for 33 years. ABC News and ABC TV Shows will promote the Globalist Left's agenda, making Goldenson one of the most influential opinion molders of the 20th century.

*Like Sarnoff, Meyer, Paley and Sulzberger before him, Leonard Goldenson's smiling liars at ABC News have inflicted enormous damage on several generations of brainwashed Americans.*

*1977: ABC's inflammatory Blockbuster mini-series, 'Roots', would instill a suicidal "White Guilt Complex" in the minds of millions of Americans.*

# WOUND # 21: 1954
## The Decline & Sudden Death of Senator Joe McCarthy

### What Happened?

Working behind the scenes, President Eisenhower helps Left Democrats and the Globalist-Marxist media to end Senator McCarthy's Senate investigation into the Marxist-Globalist subversion of America. The Establishment destroys McCarthy's reputation and finally kills the heroic Senator in an apparent poisoning in 1957.

### Consequence

The subversive American Left *(Communists / Progressives / Globalists)* survive, regroup, and grow stronger than ever. With McCarthy having been destroyed and vilified by "historians", the Marxists, knowing that they would never be seriously challenged again, now operate openly as self-described "progressives" and "liberals". Soviet archives and declassified US Army Intelligence documents have long since vindicated McCarthy's claims.

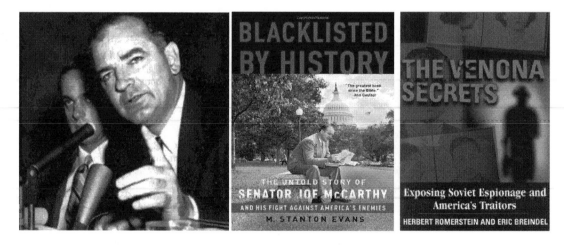

*'Blacklisted by History'* by M. Stanton Evans and 'The Venona Secrets' by Breindel & Romerstein prove that McCarthy was right, after all!

## WOUND # 22: 1963
## The Assassination of President John F Kennedy

### What Happened?

President Kennedy (JFK) is allegedly assassinated by "a lone gunman", an alleged Marxist named Lee Harvey Oswald. Oswald, **who himself will be assassinated days later**, claims to have been set up as a "patsy".

### Consequence

With the anti-Communist, pro-business JFK gone, the Democrat Party falls under the complete and permanent control of the radical Globalist Left. The new President *(Lyndon Baines Johnson)* will trick America into the planned disaster of the Vietnam War and unleash a tsunami of welfare spending.

In the Middle East, an emboldened Israel continues with the aggression and nuclear bomb-making that JFK was determined to stop.

*1 & 2: After Kennedy is clearly shot in the chest and face - not in the back of the head as the 'official story' goes - LBJ is sworn in as the new President.*

*3: Two days later, the 'fall guy" - Lee Harvey Oswald - is shot and killed on National TV by Jack Ruby. While in prison, Ruby himself dies under mysterious circumstances just three years later.*

# WOUND # 23: 1963- 1973
## Feminism / The "Women's Liberation Movement"

## What Happened?

Marxist Academics and the mass media propaganda machine convince millions of gullible young women that marriage and motherhood are tools of male-dominated "capitalist" oppression.

## Consequence

As the traditional male and female relationship is redefined as adversarial, growing marital discord leads to a sharp increase in divorce rates, broken families, broken lives, and damaged children. Millions of misled women - who chose career over family and conflict over cooperation - will end up old, lonely, childless, miserable, and hooked on anti-depressants. The Women's Liberation Movement was a slow motion CIA time-bomb intended to kill the tradition American family unit by taking mothers out of their homes, away from their children, and often into the beds of co-workers.

*Marxist Betty Friedan's "The Feminine Mystique" is hyped to the stars by the Left media. Family-wrecking feminism "liberates" women from home and family so that they can become overworked taxpaying economic units instead.*

# WOUND # 24: 1964
## The Civil Rights Act

## What Happened?

With the Marxist agitator Martin Luther King near his side, LBJ signs the Civil Rights Act into law. The Act forbids *privately-owned* businesses from discriminating against customers and prospective employees based on race, sex or national origin.

## Consequence

Under the power-grabbing guise of "anti-racism", the Civil Rights Act establishes the dangerous and destructive precedents that the Federal Government controls your private business and can dictate whatever it wants. The concerns of those who oppose the Civil Rights Act, such as Senator and 1964 Presidential candidate Barry Goldwater (R-AZ), are dismissed as "paranoid". Seeing how modern day bakery owners are now being put out of business for refusing to bake and deliver cakes for homosexual weddings, it is now obvious that Goldwater was right. **The intrusive power of the Federal Government is out-of-control.**

*Barry Goldwater was right when he warned of the longer-term dangers of giving Federal "do-gooders" too much power.*

*And so was Thomas Jefferson when he wrote:*
***"I would rather be exposed to the inconveniences attending too much liberty than those attending too small a degree of it."***

## What Happened?

Riding high after his landslide election victory of 1964; President Johnson (LBJ) and a very liberal Democrat Congress institute a series of social welfare schemes. These include Medicare *(for Seniors)*, Medicaid *(mainly for single mothers and kids)*, and Food Stamps.

## Consequence

LBJ's schemes have since turned many elderly and poor people into permanent government dependency cases and permanent Democrat voters. Far from alleviating poverty, the anti-family Great Society increased poverty by rewarding out-of-wedlock birth mothers with a care free lifestyle. **Medicare and Medicaid are two of the largest and fastest growing items in the out-of-control Federal Budget of today.**

*1: Along with America's bloated Defense budget and FDR's Social Security scheme, LBJ's welfare schemes are bankrupting America.*

*2: Johnson's Great Society entraps Americans, and makes them believe it is for their own good.*

*3: LBJ's kids: a generational dependency*

# WOUND # 26: 1965 - 1974
## The "Sexual Revolution"

## What Happened?

All at once, the traditional mores and standards which governed sexual conduct for 1000's of years are overthrown and dismissed as "religious hang ups". The new degeneracy is heavily promoted by Hollywood and Academia.

## Consequence

The combination of declining moral standards and LBJ's financial incentives for out-of-wedlock births leads to an explosion of fatherless children. As of 2013, 50% all children born in America are to single mothers, many of whom must rely upon Medicaid and Food Stamps.

Another consequence of the "sexual revolution" is the normalization of adultery, which contributes heavily to 50% divorce rates of America. **As the essential institution of the nuclear family disappears; the all-mighty State steps in to provide the trillion-dollar "safety net" that strong families and Churches once did.**

*1: CIA connected Cosmopolitan Magazine pushes the sexual revolution to the limit, and still does.*

*2 & 3: Corrupted degenerates influenced by 'The Kinsey Report' overturn 1000's of years of traditional mores, with devastating consequences for American society.*

## WOUND # 27: 1965
## The Voting Rights Act

### What Happened?

The lie that Blacks were being denied "the right to vote" is used as the pretext for extending "Voting Rights" to illiterates, morons, and non-English speakers. The use of literacy tests and basic civic exams to screen out idiots is abolished.

### Consequence

LBJ and his Democrat Party steer millions of illiterate, non-English speaking, and extreme low IQ voters into the Left's political camp, and onto the welfare rolls. Political power is exchanged for free bread, free housing and free heath care as the working middle class is squeezed to pay for it all.

*LBJ and the phony Martin Luther King collaborated on the Voting Rights Scam. As a result, even retarded people and morons get to vote themselves the wealth of the productive class.*

## What Happened?

Immigration quotas are dramatically shifted away from Europeans in favor of "Third World" immigration.

## Consequence

LBJ does it again! Millions of poor and less-educated immigrants are herded into the Democrat political camp and made dependent upon Government. The Left skillfully utilizes the new "diversity" and "multi-culturalism" as weapons to divide the public and agitate the population against Whites.

*1: With 90% of Americans being of European ancestry, the nation is deemed to be "too White". LBJ's signing of the Immigration Act is intended to eventually make European Whites a minority and then extinct altogether.*

*2: The Marxist War on the White American male is real, as Newsweek's mocking & shocking anti-White cover from 2011 proves.*

## WOUND # 29:
## 1966-1974:  The "Hippies"

### What Happened?

In justifiably rebelling against the war and Johnson's Draft, many naive and college students fall into the clever Marxist trap of rebelling against everything else that America stands for as well.

### Consequence

In the eyes of these rebellious, long-haired, drug-using, sex-crazed "hippies", the entire "system" needed to be torn down and replaced with a Utopian "One World".

In later years, many of the hippies will grow up and become decent, loyal Americans. But the hard core radicalized hippies do not. They will cut their hair, put on suits, and work to subvert America from within. **Aging hippies are still crazy; and they now rule America with an iron fist!**

*1: 1960's / 70's Hippies: Future President Bill Clinton (1993-2000) and Hillary Clinton*

*2: Black Power advocate Eric Holder (Obama's first Attorney General)*

36

## WOUND # 30: 1970
## The Environmental Protection Agency is Established

### What Happened?

A new government cabinet department, charged with powers to "protect the environment", is established.

### Consequence

Unnecessary, excessive, and dictatorial environmental regulations have rendered many American businesses unable to compete with foreign counterparts. Along with heavy taxation and frivolous litigation, EPA regs, often based upon "junk science", have either forced American business to close their operations, or forced them to relocate overseas.

Citing the **hoax** of "Global Warming", the EPA today is driving up electricity rates and killing jobs by waging war on the coal industry.

*The supposedly "conservative" Nixon greatly expanded the size and destructive power of the Federal government.*

# WOUND # 31: 1973
## The End of the Gold Standard

## What Happened?

Under pressure to pay for LBJ's 'Great Society" and the Vietnam War, Republican President Nixon severs the final linkage between Gold and the U.S. Dollar.

## Consequence

The Federal Government and the Federal Reserve are now unchained. Free of the anchor of having to partially link US Dollars to physical Gold, the spenders and lenders can perpetually flood America, and the world, with as many debased paper debt-dollars as needed to support the modern welfare and warfare states.

The inflation rate quickly spikes and continues to rise throughout the 1970's. The media blames the rising prices on "the Arab Oil Embargo", and the gullible public believes it!

*After Nixon shocked conservatives by removing the partial gold backing of the dollar, it became easier for the government to run up huge deficits with the Fed's newly printed debt-money. **This is what causes price inflation!***

# WOUND # 32: 1979
## The Department of Education Is Established

## What Happened?

Democrat President Jimmy Carter establishes the useless Department of Education.

## Consequence

The Department of Education has since grown into a $90 Billion per year monstrosity that actually *impedes* true education. **Its tragic legacy is the ever-worsening corruption of local school curriculums with Marxist propaganda aimed at impressionable young minds.**

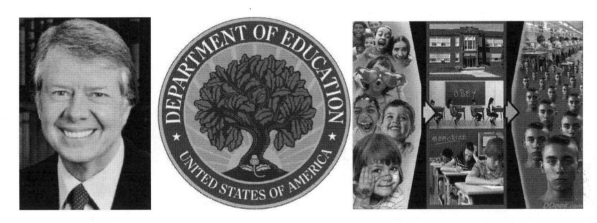

*Jimmy Carter's Education Department promotes a system in which children are transformed into non-thinking Communist robots.*

# WOUND # 33: 1980's
## The Rise of the "Neo-Conservatives"

## What Happened?

A group of Marxist-Jewish intellectuals - claiming to have recently "converted" to conservatism - are embraced and welcomed into the ranks of the classic, limited-government, constitutional conservatives.

## Consequence

With the helping hype of the Globalist Left media, the once influential conservative faction of the Republican Party is pushed aside for good by "ex-Marxist" interloping "neo cons". After completing the 'Trojan Horse' takeover of conservatism, ever-warmongering 'Israel Firster' neo-cons like Irving Kristol, Richard Perle, Charles Krauthammer, and Norman Podhoretz will water down and misdirect the true conservative movement into permanent political irrelevancy.

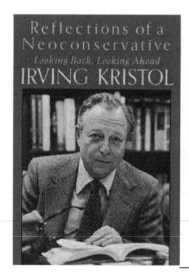

From top left: Albert Wohlstetter, Oded Yinon, Richard Perle, William Kristol, Robert Kagan, David Wurmser, Paul Wolfowitz, Joseph Lieberman, William Safire, Eliot Cohen, David Frum, Norman Podhoretz, Kenneth Adelman, Charles Krauthammer, Benjamin Netanyahu, Philip Zelikow, Elliott Abrams, Lewis "Scooter" Libby, Douglas Feith and Bernard Lewis.

*1: Irving Kristol, The "GodFather" of Zionist Neo-Conservatism, is an "ex-Communist".*

*2: Jewish Neo-Con influence will eventually lead to the disastrous Iraq War of 2003-2010. In 2015, their sights are set on Iran, Syria and Russia.*

## WOUND # 34: 1985
## Sumner Redstone *(born Murray Rothstein)* Buys MTV

### What Happened?

The popular music video station falls into the hands of a Globalist Zionist.

### Consequence

MTV transitions away from innocent music videos and begins promoting heavy sexual content and degenerate 'Hip Hop'. Redstone's MTV then expands into "news", "documentaries", and "reality shows", all of which contain a leftward, mildly pornographic, and pro homosexual flavor.

The immensely popular MTV has corrupted both the morals, and political judgment of an entire generation. Compared to today's younger crowd, the hippies of the 1960's seem like Victorian Era prudes! It is impossible to underestimate the mental and moral damage that Redstone's VIACOM *(which also owns CBS, Nickelodeon, and Univision)*, has done to the America's *(and Europe's)* youth.

*The pornographic "twerking" whore Miley Cyrus and the degenerates of 'Jersey Shore' - brought to your children by dirty old Sumner Redstone (Rothstein).*

41

## What Happened?

**The Fairy Tale:** Inexperienced Arab college kids, armed with "box-cutters" and directed by an elusive cave-dweller manage to evade the entire US Defense and Intelligence apparatus and skillfully crash hijacked airplanes into buildings, causing the Twin Towers of New York to turn into instant powder while killing 3000 Americans.

## Consequence

The pre-planned over reaction to "9/11" leads to deadly and costly trillion dollar wars, perpetual trillion dollar defense / war budgets, the establishment of the all mighty Department of Homeland Security and the liberty-destroying PATRIOT and National Defense Authorization Acts. These ominous developments have set the stage for an eventual martial law scenario in America.

*1: President George Bush (with bullhorn) uses the 9/11 attacks to initiate wars for Globalism and Zionism while radically expanding the power and size of the Federal Government.*

*2:* **Osama Bin Laden:**

*"I stress that I have not carried out this act, which appears to have been carried out by individuals (within the United States secret government) with their own motivation."*

## What Happened?

Within weeks of taking office, President Obama and his Democrat-controlled Congress pushed through an automatically renewing Federal budget with a historic **$1.6 Trillion deficit.**

## Consequence

Because of a little known procedural changes instituted by President Bill Clinton during the 1990's, Obama does not have to submit an annual budget if he doesn't want to. Indeed, Obama has not submitted any budgets since his original 2009 monstrosity.

Obama's 2009 "baseline" is thus set in stone and automatically increases every year via "continuing resolutions" and by "raising the debt ceiling". The annual Obama deficits of $1 Trillion to $1.5 Trillion are "the new normal" now as a divided and weak Republican Congress lacks the votes *(and the will-power)* to stop Obama's suicidal accumulation of debt.

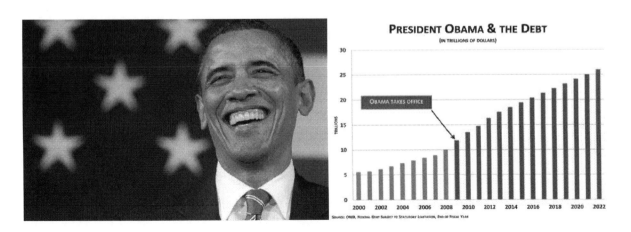

*Obama laughs as he destroys America. His deficit spending makes FDR and LBJ seem like conservatives.*

## WOUND # 37: 2010
## The Affordable Care Act *(aka "ObamaCare)*

### What Happened?

After using the emotional pretext of providing health-care for those who cannot afford it, President Obama and his Democrat Congress use procedural tricks to impose a 2000 page monstrosity upon a suspicious American public.

### Consequence

As of 2015, the private health care component of "ObamaCare" is already imploding before our eyes. Millions of Americans have already lost their health care coverage. Many millions more will either join them, or be forced to pay the skyrocketing premiums and deductibles of the new government scheme.

This unfolding disaster is deliberately engineered so that the government can eventually step in and monopolize the entire health care system altogether. **Massive new taxes, long waits, rationing, substandard care, and universal dependency upon the State are certain to be the future hallmarks of American medicine.**

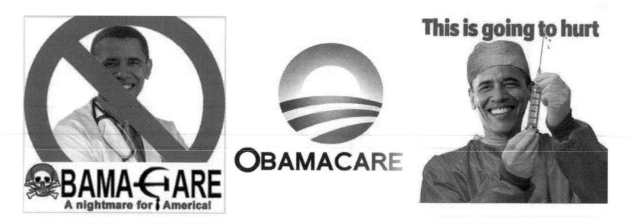

*It's not about providing "free" health care. It's about **CONTROL**!*

# WOUND # 38: 2012
## Obama Endorses Homosexual Marriage, Adoption & Trans-Genderism

## What Happened?

Believed by many to be a homosexual himself, Obama made history by affirming not only his support of "same sex marriage", but also for homosexual adoption, transgender lifestyles, and "age appropriate" sex education for kindergartners *(with a homosexual twist no doubt)*.

## Consequence

The final remnants of traditional morality and self control have now been uprooted for good. Homosexuality is no longer merely "tolerated", and no longer merely "accepted". Indeed, it is now **glorified!** Soon after Obama's public affirmation, individual States began legalizing "same sex marriage." Even conservatives have dropped their resistance against "the tide of history".

We can only imagine what social havoc the next generation of morally illiterate, overly-sexualized, and homosexually-saturated children will wreak upon our "anything goes" society in the coming years.

Can "tolerance" of pedophilia and bestiality be far behind?

*America the insane! Obama is pushing the homosexual agenda as hard and fast as he can. Just like ancient Rome!*

## WOUND # 39: 2012
## Republicans Allow the Obama Voter Fraud

### What Happened?

The inner-city, pro-Obama vote fraud of November 2012 is far more extensive and bolder than any previous such case in American history. **Republican observers are literally thrown out of Black voting precincts.** Some Democrat precincts report 100% turnout! Others register absolutely 0 votes for the Republican Mitt Romney vs 1000's of votes for Obama.

### Consequence

By refusing to contest the massive and historic fraud which took place under Obama's protection, the cowardly Republicans have surrendered America to the Marxist radicals within. For fear of being labeled "racist", a colossal crime goes unchallenged and a dangerous new precedent is established.

There is now no opposition to King Obama, at all. All that is left now for Obama, or his successor, is to deal the final death blow to what was once "the land of the free, and the home of the brave."

*1- The gutless Republican Mitt Romney and his equally gutless running mate, Paul Ryan, refused to challenge the massive, self-evident Democrat vote fraud of 2012.*

*2- Philadelphia man **openly** boasts on CNN, "I voted twice."*

## What Happened?

America's southern border with Mexico has been porous for quite some time. During the Presidencies of Democrat Bill Clinton and Republican George W. Bush, the invasion of illegal aliens had reached unprecedented level of 1.3 million per year. Now, under Obama, the numbers are no longer even known as **the Department of Homeland Security is actively facilitating the transport of the aliens to America.**

## Consequence

The cost to the American taxpayer to feed, house, incarcerate, provide medical care and public education for these aliens will be astronomical. Many criminals are also crossing the border unmolested. Americans who complain about the invasion are denounced by the media as "racist" or "xenophobic".

These invaders will indeed be voting in American elections, obviously for Left Democrats. In years to come, the voting coalition of amnestied illegal aliens, combined with millions of legal Third World immigrants, will make the Marxist Democrats unstoppable. It has already happened in previously conservative California.

*Here come MILLIONS of new Democrat welfare voters!*

# CLOSING STATEMENT / FUTURE WOUNDS

So there you have them; the top 40 deadly wounds which constitute the murder of America. Perhaps there are a few more than could be added, and a few that could be dropped, but you get the point. It is said that Rome wasn't built in a day. Nor was it destroyed in a day. The same holds true for America.

This author wishes he could offer you a way out, a 'rah-rah' motivational speech about "taking the country back"; but it appears that the mental and moral cancer of Globalist liberalism has metastasized; and that a few more death blows may be coming soon. The architects of The New World Order aren't finished with us yet.

Some possibilities:

- The provocation of a war with Russia and China
- Engineered race riots and/or civil war
- Debt-driven hyper-inflationary economic collapse
- Epic Stock Market collapse
- Staged terror attacks to be blamed on _____?
- Martial Law

The best we can all do now is inform ourselves and prepare ourselves for some very interesting times ahead.

# *Read the full length illustrated works of M S King available via Amazon and Kindle.*

King is also the webmaster of **TomatoBubble.com** and author of:

- ***The Bad War****: The Story Never Taught About World War 2 (245 p)*
- ***The War Against Putin****: What the Government-Media Complex Isn't Telling You About Russia. (110 p)*
- ***The Real Roosevelts****: What Ken Burns Didn't Tell You (106 p)*
- ***Mein Side of the Story****: Key World War 2 Addresses of Adolf Hitler (130 p)*

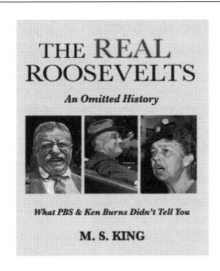

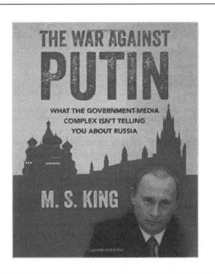

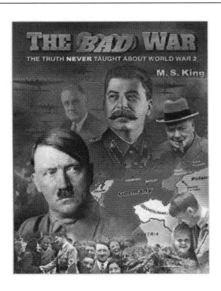

*

95103927R00028

Made in the USA
Columbia, SC
04 May 2018